The
Xenophobe's® Guide to
The Californians

Anthony Marais

D1513857

Oval Books

Published by Oval Books
335 Kennington Road
London SE11 4QE
United Kingdom

Telephone: +44 (0)20 7582 7123
Fax: +44 (0)20 7582 1022
E-mail: info@ovalbooks.com

Editor – Catriona Tulloch Scott
Series Editor – Anne Tauté

Cover designer – Jim Wire, Quantum
Printer – Cox & Wyman Ltd
Producer – Oval Projects Ltd

Xenophobe's® is a Registered
Trademark.

ISBN: 1-902825-20-9

Contents

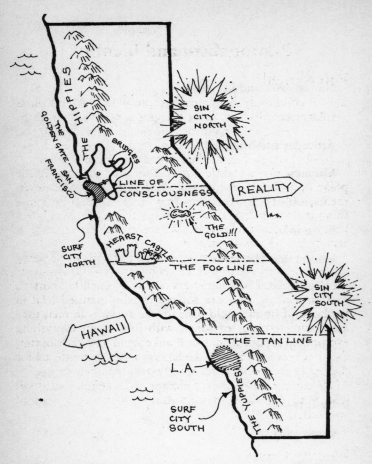

Of 268 million Americans, 32 million live in California, compared with 18 million in New York State, 3 million in Oklahoma, 15 million in Florida, 29 million Canadians and 92 million Mexicans.

California is bigger than Germany and Belgium put together. The distance from north to south (as the Roadrunner speeds) is equivalent to travelling from London (England) to Venice (the one in Italy, not the Beach).

Nationalism and Identity

Forewarned

It is a commonly held misconception that Californians are American. Indeed, most foreigners believe them to be the televised embodiment of Americana, and yet the real Americans, the other 88%, can do no more than hopelessly shake their heads when asked about these people.

Californians are different. Culturally, they form the polar opposite of Europeans, Americans and often even themselves. There are myths that credit the sun or something magical in the golden soil for the mysterious effect California has on people. Whatever the attraction, it seduces all who come its way.

Some people are eccentric, others contradictory, many are radical and even more are conventional. Californians are delusional. Like characters out of Dashiell Hammett's *Maltese Falcon*, they are forever chasing painted lead in the hope of finding gold beneath the surface. In fact, they are completely out of touch with just about everything except their image. And, like Frankenstein and his monster, they have come to believe the fantasies they've produced for the rest of the world, often at the expense of their sanity.

Welcome xenophobe! Welcome to a people who will take your fear of foreigners and turn it into a fear of yourself.

Identity Crises

Of the many delusions that Californians harbour, first and foremost is the delusion that they're Californian. The only real Californians have names like Chumash, Miwok, Yurok and Pomo, their forebears having occupied the land for at least 9,000 years. Today the term 'native Californian' encompasses just about anyone from first-generation immigrants to name-changers and confidence-tricksters. The term 'Californian' – inasmuch as it defines a race or even a nationality – does not exist. Addressing someone as a 'Californian' is like sending a letter to 'Hollywood', which is actually not a city, but a section of the city of Los Angeles. As the old saying goes, 'California isn't a state, it's a state of mind'. To claim to be a Californian is to be Californian.

The current demography of Californians can be divided roughly into 40% White, 35% Hispanic, 10% Black, 10% Asian and 5% Everyone Else. Whatever their ethnic origins, Californians are 100% dreamers, always planning their next stunt, always on the brink of a new escapade, and this is ultimately the criterion that divides them from the rest of the world.

How Others See Them

By turning on the television. Ever since Laurel and Hardy, Charlie Chaplin and Buster Keaton came on the scene, the Californian has been a highly visible breed. Even in the remotest corners of the globe, no television is without the whitened smiles, lifted faces and bouncing bathing suits of the West Coast elite. And no-one is without a preconceived, media-based opinion of these people they've never met.

Adjectives abound to describe the libertines of 'La-La Land'. What outsider doesn't get a feeling of satisfaction when he or she hears a Californian called plastic, shallow, brain-baked, or freaky? After all, this is exactly how they are seen on television. For the most part these labels are true, but for the 98% of Californians who will never look into the lens of a movie camera, they describe only a fraction of their personalities.

Many Europeans see Americans as loud, childish and overly extroverted. This is how many Americans see Californians. In the wake of a temporary recession and with their spirit of conquest, adventure and the hunt for cheap housing, Californians have started resettling in the Northwest and Southwest United States. This contact with Californians has helped to fortify most of the stereotypes the rest of America thought were true but weren't quite sure about. The general consensus of non-Californians is that Californians are all crazy. Hence:

Q: How is California like a bowl of granola?
A: Once you take out the flakes and fruits, all you're left with are the nuts.

How They See Others

Through very dark sunglasses. Californians suffer from and enjoy a healthy amount of ethnocentrism. Nesting themselves on a strip of homeland buttressed by the Pacific Ocean on one side and palisaded by the Sierra Nevada Mountains on the other hasn't helped matters.

Since the beginning, Californians have practised a cultural isolationism in a country founded on political isolationism. In other words, they've cut themselves off from just about everybody. In doing so, Californians have created a complete world for themselves: the songs on the radio recount the freeways you are driving on, the TV sitcoms depict your situation, the movies show the beach you were at earlier that day, and the novels describe coffee shops you often visit. Even your textbook describes research carried out and published not far from the lecture hall where you are learning about it. All these things help to cement their delusion that Californians sit at the centre of the universe. And it's from this high perch that they see the rest of the world.

Special Relationships

Not without a 'pre-nup', thanks. Californians have special relationships with just about everybody, even if they only last a few minutes.

Though they often don't admit it, there are many in the shallow West who fear the Deep South. This 'hillbilly-phobia' often surfaces in Hollywood films which inevitably misrepresent those who speak with a drawl and sing with a twang. The irony is that many Californians came from the South (cities like Bellflower still have horse ranches and feed stores). LA in particular received a flood of Southern and Mid-West immigrants during the Depression.

But ever since the New Yorkers moved in, started knocking up chic 'tract' homes (identical houses built on a tract of land) beneath their new 'Hollywoodland' sign, building the first movie studio on Sunset and Gower, bringing with them hordes of bagel-eating go-getters with exotic East European accents, California just hasn't been the same.

The result of this migration has been a kind of sibling rivalry between the New Yorkers and the Californians whereby the older is eternally shaking its head at the careless exploits of the upstart younger. Watch any Woody Allen movie to hear quotes like "Sun is bad for you" and "I'm getting my chronic Los Angeles nausea again".

Californians love to remind themselves how miserable their lives would have been had they stuck it out East, in the cold. They see the New Yorkers as highly strung stress cases. A typical Californian comment is: "New York is the only city in the world where you can get run down deliberately on the sidewalk by a pedestrian."

Probably the most special relationship Californians share with any other group is their symbiotic bond with the Mexicans. This can be somewhat confusing to the outsider because the 35% of Californians who are of Hispanic descent should not be confused with 'real' Mexicans – namely, those who have not been affected by the delusion.

Many Californians are afflicted with a warped form of elitism regarding the Mexicans who cross the border in the hope of a fistful of dollars. These people, bearers of the American dream, make up the throngs of gardeners, maids, busboys, and itinerant field labourers who indeed make the state run, but suffer under the snobby prejudice of immigrants who got there a few years earlier.

How They See Other Californians

Blinded by the sun, clouded by the fog. There are two kinds of Californians, a statement which does not refer to race or creed, but to what side of Hearst Castle* you are from. That is to say, Northern or Southern California. The visitor may think they all look alike, but Northern and Southern Californians know they are really two different breeds.

Crudely summarised, the Northern Californians see themselves as the politically aware, down-to-earth conveyors of culture, and the Southern Californians see themselves as the stylish, politically potent producers of culture. Northern Californians tend to be Liberal Democrats, whereas Southern Californians gravitate towards conservative Republicanism.

The Northern Californians see the Southern Californians as everything evil in the world. They're the shallow, drunken, conservative, close-minded yuppies that Berkeley mothers threaten their daughters with when

* The extraordinary turreted mansion of newspaper baron William Randolph Hearst upon which Xanadu, the fabled home of Citizen Kane, is modelled.

they come home wearing too much make-up. According to most Northern Californians, there's nothing wrong with Southern California that a rise in sea level wouldn't cure.

The Southern Californians basically don't see the Northern Californians at all. It's rumoured that there's a city somewhere in all that rain and fog.

How They See Themselves

As often as possible and wherever a mirror can be found. Why not? What other state's citizens have an element – californium (Cf, atomic number 98) – named after them? Who else can lay claim to the Martini and Chop Suey?

More immigrants settle in California than any other state in the United States – more than one third of the country's total in 1994. Even the Russians tried to colonise California, but not realising a good property deal when they had one, they went back home in 1841 when the supply of seals ran out, leaving behind them the town of Sebastopol, the Russian River and Fort Ross. They sold Fort Ross to John Sutter for $30,000 – but he only ever paid them $10,000.

No other state is more populous – today there are over 32 million Californians. In fact, one out of eight Americans is Californian – and as far as the Californians are concerned, seven out of eight wish they were. The California Department of Finance projects that by the year 2040, 63 million people will reside in California. Facts like these help Californians convince themselves they are special. While others may see Californians in comparatives, they see themselves in superlatives.

Whatever their differences, Northern and Southern Californians share a sense of being progressive. The idea is simple: the farther west you go, the deeper you penetrate the frontier, and thus the farther away you get from puri-

10

tanical New England. The outsider should remember that most Californians don't go back more than a generation and subconsciously see themselves in a similar position to a new Chief Executive Officer or a 'rookie' (newcomer). They've just arrived, and feel the responsibility to prove themselves. Everyone back home is expecting it. In the film version of *Sunset Boulevard*, William Holden is not drawn to the ageing Gloria Swanson out of a love of money but a fear of having to return to his old life in Ohio. Thus, under the pressure to perform, Californians see themselves as resourceful trendsetters. And what better tool than the media to prove to the world they are right.

If Americans are good, Californians are better. And if Americans are bad, Californians are still better. How does one know that? Ask a Californian.

Character

Don't Worry, Be Happy

Many foreigners interpret the gregarious spontaneity of Californians as shallow or superficial. It is important that the visitor realise this is entirely true. When you are at the supermarket and the checker cheerfully asks "How're you doing?", this usually does not include your being dumped by your lover who was supposed to pay the rent this month. However, what many outsiders tend to miss out on is the philosophy behind the superficiality. The happy-go-lucky approach to life is critical to the delusion. Tell the king he's naked and the party is over.

It works like this: if enough people pretend to be happy, they can cause a chain reaction which in turn makes them 'become' happy, or at least puts them in a good mood. Life is too short to be in a bad mood. And besides, if you can exude enough happiness, you might actually get paid for it. Anything can happen.

Northern Californians express their West Coast Cool not so much with ecstatic outbursts as with a laid-back savoir-faire – the kind that produced one of the all-time greatest jazz hits, *Take Five* (by Dave Brubeck, a native Californian). But beware: these are often the most deceiving of Californians, for that chuckling guy in the Hawaiian shirt over there is actually a world-renowned molecular biologist. And his freaked-out looking friend has just won a Nobel prize.

Californians chat up the checker and tell her to "Have a nice day" even though they are living under enough stress to crush an average man or woman.

Why do they do this? The reason is really quite simple: the weather. Ask any Oxford professor to take off his gown and put on a Hawaiian shirt and watch the personality change. Also keep in mind that the West Coast is the newest part of America, and many of the cultural mores and restrictions that inhibit societal freedom on the East Coast and in Europe have not had the chance to develop.

So relax; open your mind to all possibilities, and remember it's not what you know but who you know. So smile as much as possible, you never know who you might meet.

Let's Be Friends

The Californians' 'sunny smiles' may best be summed up in the following true story. It involves a New Englander's attempt to find a relative's house in the condo-grafted hills of Orange County.

Already awe-struck by the descent across Los Angeles, and exhausted by the one-hour-fifteen-minute drive from LAX (pronounced el-ay-ex) – Los Angeles International Airport – to Mission Viejo, the visitor got lost. The last time she visited, there were about 50 homes on the side of the dusty hill. Now there were about 650.

After what seemed like an eternity, the determined Easterner got as far as the cul-de-sac where her sister supposedly lived. This already deserved merit for there were only four different models amongst those 650 houses. Just as she was about to collapse in the heat, she noticed a man watering his lawn. She called to him in desperation and asked for help. And no sooner did she open her mouth than she experienced it: California friendliness. With a beaming, toothpaste-promoting smile, the man dropped his hose and jogged to the rescue.

Within minutes she was out of her car and being guided to a large, cold glass of lemonade and the pearly whites of Mrs Golden-Coast. Amidst chuckles and jokes and pats on the back, the New Englander explained that she had forgotten her sister's address. They said not to worry, their door was always open. They even offered to put her up for a night should she not find her sister. So as the 'guest' from 'that quaint and historical corner of the country' sipped her lemonade, the friendliest people in the world thumbed through the phone book in search of the missing sister. The man found the name and burst out laughing: "Why, that's our next-door neighbour!"

Californians usually don't meet their neighbours until there's a fire. Otherwise they are too busy being friendly to bother.

Dress for Excess

The Californian by nature does not recognise moderation. This is put away with the winter coats upon arrival. Sometime in the 1850s, the gold miners started a tradition of trying to get something for nothing and then, when they did, blowing it as quickly as possible. The pattern survives to this day with the only change being property value instead of gold. The Californians live by the 'more is more' philosophy. They lead the United States in both personal income and consumer expenditure. "Shop till you drop" is the battle cry of Orange County. If you've got it, flaunt it. It will help inspire the others who follow in your path.

This behaviour can make life complicated for the visitor because what you see is not always what you get with Californians. It is quite possible that the Tom Selleck look-alike who just drove up in the brand new Porsche, peeking over his $500 LA Eye-Wear sunglasses, will drive home tonight to a humble one-bedroom flat in the low-rent district. In fact, the car is on lease and the sunglasses were borrowed from a friend. Two weeks ago he was on foot – and on the lam – but he recently landed a job as key grip on a low-budget horror movie.

External appearance is vital to Californians. Clothing is a statement. Neutral does not exist. Even the apparently easy-going hippies of Mendocino garb themselves in funky style. In south central LA, the colours blue or red – symbols of gang affiliation – are taken more seriously than political parties in other parts of the world. In Orange County, girls wear shirts stating "Charge it!". In Berkeley they state "Smoke it!". The character of Californians is as visible as the shirts on their backs.

Carpe Diem

Most Californians grow up with the fantasy that they can do anything if they really want to. But while other American children lose their hope of becoming President while they are still in their teens, Californians don't give up hope of becoming something their entire lives. The consequence of this stubborn idealism is a characteristic

14

whereby the Californian is perpetually on the verge of being anything he or she wants. Every new day sees the death of one dream and the birth of two more – the roster of manic-depressive cases follows suit.

Paranoia

Some children fear the Bogeyman, others the Big Bad Wolf; little Californian boys and girls go to sleep with visions of Charles Manson coming to cut their baby out of them and write Beatles' songs on the wall with their blood. In school they are visited by police officers who teach them to walk against the traffic so they cannot be picked up and taken away by a madman. Halloween candy must be checked for glass and razor blades. The word 'hitchhiking' is synonymous with 'suicide'.

Browse any West Coast bookstore and see where the Californians' interests lie: *The Culture of Fear, Freedom from Fear, Feel the Fear and Do it Anyway* are just a few of the titles gracing the best-seller lists. Postcards show California's four seasons as Earthquakes, Riots, Mudslides and Fires.

Californians have created one of the most heterogeneous societies in the world, and yet race issues remain as hot as the asphalt in Bakersfield. In April 1992 Angelenos experienced the tragedy known alternately as The Riots or The Uprising. Sparked by widespread dissatisfaction with the acquittal of four LAPD officers who were videotaped beating a black man named Rodney King, anarchy broke out in south central Los Angeles. Businesses were looted, buildings set ablaze and passers-by dragged from their cars and beaten. And all this 'live' on television. The Californians, who already had a fear of crime, sat glued to their sets as they watched stores being broken into and robbed while the police impotently looked on. What started out as a fear of psychopaths suddenly became a fear of everyone.

Most Californians have a gold digger's fear of theft. The message they received during The Riots was that their 'claims' were unprotected. This fed their conviction that life in California is a life on the edge.

The resulting personality is that of a panophobic extrovert. The Californian has retained his love of life while simultaneously harbouring a fear of people. Party all you like, but just be careful not to get shot when you're throwing pebbles at your girlfriend's window.

Profoundly Superficial

It is possible that in that great data bank in the sky, when it came time to file the Californians, someone confused the words 'character' and 'caricature'. The girl who resembles a vapid blonde bimbette from the San Fernando Valley may be dubbed a 'Valley Girl' but in fact she really is. She is a real person trying to look like an image of a stereotype. Californians often seem to be reflections of themselves, and defining them is to step into a house of mirrors.

Because nobody is really Californian, everyone who settles there contributes equally to its personality, and no single group can claim to be more Californian than another. Indeed every new person who comes to California in a small way redefines what it means to be Californian. However, what all Californians share is a peculiar tendency to display an exaggerated mode of their former selves. For instance, a hometown star will subconsciously feel compelled to act the part once he has reached the land of opportunity.

The Californian author John Steinbeck sums it up in *East of Eden* when he observes that Californians are "a breed – selected out by accident", and poses the rhetorical question: "Do you know of any other nation that acts for ideals?"

Attitudes and Values

Wealth

The city of Los Angeles alone has a greater GNP than Australia. It has been said that if the 'really' big quake should ever hit, causing the Golden State to break off and head in the direction of Honolulu, it would be the fifth wealthiest country in the world. After all, it doesn't take a seismologist to imagine the profit generated by the computer, film and aerospace industries which sprouted up sometime after the last disheartened 'forty-niner' (gold prospector of the 1849 Gold Rush) packed his empty bags and went home.

Eking out an existence on the dried-up soil of a farm in Kansas is what the Californian has symbolically left behind. Living high on the hog is unquestionably accepted as the reward for making the move. Thus, when a shiny new stretch limousine pulls up to a shack in the slums, the neighbours don't sneer. On the contrary, it's with a smile that they watch their acquaintance enjoying his piece of the pie.

In a desert, water is a symbol of wealth, which may explain why the city of Palm Springs and its environs have more than 90 golf courses, all requiring a computer-controlled daily drenching to keep them green. This makes Canadians and other environmentally aware peoples angry; however, to the Californians it's a well-earned reward for a century of innovation. Since the beginning, Californians have aired their wealth through the 'fertilis-ing' of their barren culture. What is considered to be the best existing likeness of Chaucer in a book is not to be found in Canterbury, but in the Huntington Library in San Marino, near Pasadena. It's displayed just a few paces away from an original copy of the Gutenberg Bible. This acquisitive spirit is critically important to Californians in fostering the delusion that their Eden is Eden.

In the 1957 horror movie *Curse of the Demon*, the British occultist (Niall MacGinnis) warns the sceptical American psychologist (Dana Andrews): 'You get nothing for nothing'. To the Californian these seemingly harmless words are in fact more frightening than the demon that comes at the end of the film. Deep in the Californian psyche is the idea that you are automatically entitled to something for nothing by the simple fact of being there.

The problem with living in such a society is the constant reminder that someone got there before you. In this sense, Californians are often left feeling like outsiders in their own culture. Take a drive through Bel Air and look at the homes you'll never own. Wealth is Californian. Therefore, those who are wealthy are some-how more Californian.

Love

Californians love everything. They love books, food, talk-ing, hairdos, dogs, cars, stars and clothes. But what they love most is love itself, so much, in fact, that the word is used whenever and wherever possible. So don't be surprised when a Californian loves you on holiday, but forgets to send a postcard.

For most people, love is something intangible, not seen in daily life and difficult to find. With Californians this is not so. Love can easily be found by typing the word 'love.com' on your computer. Here, along with a drove of other dating services, the desires and aspirations of

Californians are blithely revealed to the world. Regardless of race or sex, the Golden West ideal appears to be a positive thinking millionaire who looks like a movie star and always tells the truth.

If the dream doesn't pan out, the effects of Cupid's arrow can be discussed at a 'Making Love Work' seminar or perhaps on a visit to the nearest nudist colony where classes are offered in emotional bonding for the free at heart. By day, the beach is home to families, surfers and sunbathers, but in the small hours of the morning the cold sand has served as a backdrop for many a romantic interlude. How many Californians hold memories of late night encounters on blankets before the crashing waves of the Pacific, the world will never know.

Divorce

Teased for not knowing the word 'alimony', a small girl revealed before her third-grade class that her parents were not only married but had never been married to anyone else. The teacher, who was on her sixth husband, politely told the children not to make fun of "traditional" people.

Ironically, Californian law is not so lax regarding divorce as the Californians themselves. Adultery, mental or physical cruelty, alcoholism, desertion, non-support and imprisonment are not grounds for divorce. However, insanity is, which perhaps accounts for the 50% divorce rate. If this doesn't work, a divorce can be granted on the grounds of 'irreconcilable differences'. If the lawyer's bills are too high, a mediator can be hired to help work out the knots before the meeting in the courtroom. And if that is too expensive, then try a 'DIY' divorce where you and your future ex can spend long evenings together filling out the forms.

Nothing typifies the West Coast pursuit of happiness better than the concept of the ideal divorce – the one thing that could top a perfect wedding. Whereas others struggle with the bonds of matrimony, Californians strive for bliss in separation. The idea is simple. All the love, trust and respect needed for an optimal marriage apply to an ideal divorce. The result is a family portrait resembling a large group of friends. At your high school graduation, the thought of greeting Mom and her latest male accessory and Dad with his newest female friend (either of whom may well be graduating with you) may seem unnerving, but it's what many Californians hope for in a life riddled with change.

Arguably, the high divorce rate amongst Californians is a reflection of their idealism – 'better to have loved and lost than never to have loved at all' is the consensus. The Californians like a good party. The trend amongst many is to get married quickly, make a big show of the wedding, settle into matrimony for about eight months, and then bail out upon realising you don't have the same 'EQ' (Emotional Quotient) levels.

The actress Shelly Winters nicely summed it up when she mused: "In Hollywood all marriages are happy – it's trying to live together afterwards that causes the problems." Mickey Rooney, who married eight times, once remarked: "Always get married early in the morning – that way, if it doesn't work out, you haven't wasted the whole day."

Death

Simply put, Californians don't like to die. Death is something to be avoided at all costs – and that can be a lot. Medical facilities are of the highest standard, but woe betide those who can't pay the bills. If you think it's expensive to look young, try living beyond your years.

The interest on borrowed time in California is exorbitant. Nevertheless, Californians are forever attempting to cheat Old Man Time.

One of the cleverer Californians to try was none other than Walt Disney who had himself frozen in the hope that future technology would be able to bring him back. To the chagrin of his relatives, Walt had the audacity to place his entire fortune in a trust for himself. If the refrigeration company had not gone bankrupt three years later, leaving him to thaw in a Hollywood parking lot, he might have got away with it.

Death is not so much a taboo subject as a non-existent one. It simply has no place in ethereal Californian culture. It's too real. Thus, as death approaches, the Californian fights back with a vengeance. And if it can't be bought off, tricked or avoided, then the Californian may do something extravagant, like Lillian Entwistle who in 1932 committed suicide by jumping from the 'H' in the Hollywood sign – in pursuit of fame to the bitter end. Or like Errol Flynn who reputedly met the Grim Reaper in the middle of coitus.

Nostalgia

Bewildering but true is that beneath every Californian tan is a bleeding heart. Merely mention a rusting billboard or dilapidated taco stand and watch the eyes begin to brim. Nostalgia is an unavoidable side effect of a society that ignores tradition. An innocent question as to the location of a bank can lead to a heart-wrenching reminiscence of the days of wine and roses. Yet the same person will happily accept that The Brown Derby, watering hole of the stars and symbol of Hollywood's golden era, has become a Korean karaoke bar.

In California, the culture mirrors the geophysics – both

are unstable. Bridges crumble under seismic pressure, and businesses collapse under capitalistic selection. The Californian sits in the midst of it all, grasping a Barbie doll, stricken with insecurity, dreaming of the days when Paramount was paramount, and the MGM lion roared from its own cage.

Gays

Disneyland may be the happiest place on earth, but the gayest is 450 miles to the north. The Castro district of San Francisco is home to more than 90,000 gays, and its annual Gay Parade puts to shame all but the best of the Latin American carnivals. So don't be surprised if while waiting to use a bank machine you find yourself sandwiched between a cross-dresser and a cowboy or a biker wearing chaps. This is California: a rugged frontier where men are men (and so are many women).

Hippies

If you appreciate the vegetarian section of a menu, you're right in tune with what has become a Californian standard and you have the Hippies to thank. Haight-Ashbury, Berkeley and Venice Beach produce what could be called the Golden Triangle of Hippiedom. To this day you can leave your heart in San Francisco, blow your mind in Berkeley, and then pick up the pieces in Venice.

The song says that if you're going to San Francisco, put flowers in your hair. Today that might not be enough. Perhaps a full-body tattoo, a pincushion-full of piercings, stretched earlobes and some ritual scarification would be more appropriate. Perhaps not all Californians look like hippies, but the majority thinks like them. Hippies have had a fundamental influence on the Californian character. By making tolerance and experimentation part of what it is to be Californian, they took a life-philosophy that began as alternative and made it mainstream.

Dudes

Dude is not just a word, it's a philosophy. Ironically, the word probably rode into California on the backs of 'Oakie' horses during the Dust Bowl (the Oklahoma drought of the 1930s that forced many to migrate to California). Originally it denoted a city slicker from the East who wanted to be a cowboy for a weekend. Today it's part of the sacred vernacular of the surfer and signifies a special position in Californian society.

When a Californian calls you "dude", he does not mean it's time to 'saddle 'em up and get some chuck 'n' beans'. The term is more akin to 'sir' or 'my lord', and to be referred to as "The Dude" is nothing short of being knighted. Like the cavalier, the name denotes an almost ascetic devotion to a life of anti-materialism, soul-searching and communion with nature. This is most often achieved through a long-term commitment to unemployment, television watching and surfing. It is no easy task. Most dudes don't reach the status of The Dude until at least their mid-forties.

It is perfectly possible that on a particularly bad day, without your realising how miserable you look, a dude may approach you and ask "What's up?" Stunned, you respond with "Excuse me?" With absolute sincerity, the dude will say: "You look bummed, dude – I just thought I'd tell ya we're in this thing together – Ya gotta chill out – I know what yer feelin'." Your first thought is, how could this flake who looks as if he earns less than your 14-year-old son have something to tell you. Later, just as you're falling asleep, you ask yourself when was the last time you showed someone in the street some sympathy, and you realise that The Dude is indeed at a higher level.

Religion

Californians are believers. Cynics, sceptics and atheists are advised to go directly to New York. In fact, Californians take their beliefs so seriously that many lose touch with what doesn't need to be believed, i.e. reality.

The members of Heaven's Gate thought they could ride Hale-Bopp Comet into the next world – they succeeded. On 26 March 1997, the bodies of 39 people, dressed in black with arm patches reading HEAVEN'S GATE AWAY TEAM, were found in a plush mansion in Rancho Santa Fe, near San Diego. The dead included an ex-Miss Rodeo, a former cowboy movie actor and the brother of an actress in the television series *Star Trek*. These devotees of Marshall Applewhite believed that by following him into death they would be picked up by a UFO (scheduled to arrive with the comet) that would take them to a reincarnated life on another planet. Marshall Applewhite was a devotee of Madame Blavatsky, founder of the Theosophy movement in 1875, who believed that California was to be the cradle of a new race.

The People's Temple of San Francisco believed itself to be fostering a "new birth of social justice". When its followers were faced with failure in the face of capitalism, they chose death. They believed so strongly, that on 18 November 1978, in the remote jungle of northwest Guyana, 909 of them committed suicide by drinking cyanide-laced Kool-Aid in the name of God and Jim Jones.

From Catholicism to Dianetics, Mennonites to Scientologists, Californians embrace, alter and create religions with the hunger of sucklings. It has been suggested that the ups and downs of the film industry and the computer industry create individuals who are prime candidates for the extremist religions that thrive so well in the West. Tom Cruise and John Travolta are examples of established figures who have taken to them in a big way. In a culture where fame and fortune are expected at the end of every resumé, fear of discontent is pandemic. This leads Californians to attempt to find meaning in the unreal world they have created. In no instance is their proclivity to delusion more apparent than in their willingness to believe they have found the answer.

For Russians, religion may be the opium of the masses. For Californians, it's their only escape.

Manners

Californians are basically relaxed regarding most forms of etiquette. Tacky clothing, sloppy table manners and inappropriate humour are quickly interpreted as easygoing and thus acceptable. In general, Californians are more interested in breaking with tradition than upholding it. Yet oddly, they like to queue. There's nothing like the pleasure of waiting an hour and forty-five minutes at one's favourite restaurant. Each party waits its turn in an impressively organised manner. Remarkably few ever try to 'take cuts'.

There can be no better example of the urge to queue than a trip to Disneyland where Californians feel right at home waiting in endless lines just to get in. Once they finally enter the park, the waiting really begins. Attractions in Disneyland are like restaurants in LA – the longer one waits, the better it feels. A new trip through outer space could have one waiting in Fantasyland for a ride in Tomorrowland.

On the Road

In every Californian there is what Disney once termed 'Mr Walker' and 'Mr Wheeler.' The former is that happy-go-lucky chap skipping out of his suburban home across a spotless driveway, down to his shiny new car parked next to the palm tree. The latter typifies the other 90% of Californians, the faceless maniac, child of Evel Knievel, breathing fire and spewing out profanities, attempting to reach Mach 5 before the signal turns red, all pedestrians being expendable. From the 'Porte Cochère' of Bullocks Wilshire (the first department store in the world designed around the automobile) to the roller-coasteresque sprawl of freeways that make up the LA of today, Californians have a passion for rapid transit.

They also have a passion for cars. This is the land of hot-rod hearses, gold Rolls Royces, grand piano Cadillacs, peach-fuzz BMWs, and hot-pink patent leather seats. Being the Roadrunner zipping freely across a desert, unhindered by cops or coyotes, is what most Californians dream about. Drag racing on Mulholland Drive to a fatal James Dean or Montgomery Clift climax is the closest Californians come to a Shakespearean end.

Highway etiquette amongst Californians is more structured than one might think. There is a complex set of unwritten rules that (although they defy the law) must be respected if one is to drive properly in the Golden State. Firstly, when starting off from an intersection, wait until all the speed zealots are through running the red light in the crossing direction. Secondly, when on the freeways (though you see seven sets of lines) remember there is only one lane: the passing lane. Thirdly, when approaching a four-way stop, slow down a bit, keeping the rhythm of your music, look for cops, and before you lose your momentum, punch the gas. This is called a 'Californian Stop'.

Obsessions

Traffic

If you find yourself stuck on a freeway flowing as quickly as tar through a straw, being asphyxiated by the fumes of a sea of exhaust pipes in front of you, and suddenly notice that the guy in the next lane is about to shoot you with a .45-calibre Dirty Harry Special, you are actually experiencing three of the Californians' obsessions at once.

Traffic to the Californian is like ice to the Eskimo: it slows you down, you're surrounded by it, it's often a nuisance, but it just wouldn't be home without it. Coming to a complete stop on a 12-lane freeway with the sun glaring in your eyes to the tune of 'Life in the Fast Lane' is an essential part of the California experience. When Angelenos talk about the "Orange Crush", they are not speaking of a soft drink or football game, they are talking about where the 91, 605, 22 and 55 freeways meet in the city of Orange. From the first on-ramp to the last off-ramp, their motorised, cloverleaf world stretches itself across no less than 464 square miles (746 square kilometres) of land. This means that to get some more toilet paper often entails driving to a megastore with a Disneyland-sized parking lot.

Los Angeles has earned the title of America's number one waster of time in traffic. Angelenos spend no less than 82 hours a year stuck in traffic jams. The frustration that results has given the world the term 'road rage'.

Traffic-angst permeates all levels of life for Californians. When meeting an attractive man in a bar, once he has been cleared astrologically, it must be established if the possible relationship is "commutable". Nothing is worse than falling for someone with bad freeway connections.

Smog

There are theories that suggest Pasadena no longer exists. After all, no-one has actually seen it for at least 22 years. It has been said that California possesses a special light: a glowing radiance basking in the listless air-currents between desert and ocean. This is true. It came with the introduction of some 20 million cars to the air providing some of the most beautiful brown sunsets you will ever see.

The news sent back by journalist Charles Nordhof to New York in 1873 was: "The purity of the air in Los Angeles is remarkable. The air, when inhaled, gives to the individual a stimulus and vital force which only an atmosphere so pure can ever communicate." Today, when inhaled, the air gives to the individual a stimulus and vital force which only a smoker of three packs a day can ever communicate. The comic Vaudevillian Joe Frisco put it thus: "Hollywood is the only place where you can wake up in the morning and hear the birds coughing in the trees."

Crime

The most disturbing of the Californian delusions to come true has been their love and fear of crime. The Californians nothing short of deify their most wanted. Names like Charles Manson, Sirhan Sirhan, the Ramirez Brothers, the Zodiac Killer, the Hillside Strangler and the Night Stalker send a chill down the Californian's spine. It has been suggested that a critical factor in becoming a serial killer in America is coming from the Mid-West and going to San Francisco. This fatal combination has produced some of the Californians' favourite psychopaths.

There are in fact few Californians who do not pass a certain portion of their day discussing the apocalyptic proportions of crime in their community. However, it is sometimes difficult to hear them over the thunder of police helicopters overhead, the television howling the daily death toll, the radio blaring anthems to the lawless, and the sirens screaming by. Just as Alcatraz and its prison are central to San Francisco Bay, crime is central to Californians' lives. Ironically crime rates have been falling in California, yet it is not only a favourite topic of film and television, but an actual element of the daily routine. Many Californians can claim to have handled urban weapons, to have heard gunshots at night, to have witnessed police brutality and to have known victims of violence. And these are the respectable ones.

The obsession with crime is amplified by news reports of violence which compete for your attention by depicting the events in ever increasing graphic detail. The latest trend has been 'live' reportage (a.k.a. 'real TV') in which the news cameras are present at the scene as the crime is actually taking place. This trend has led to 'live action' drug raids, high-speed pursuits and controversial televised beatings and deaths. Simply put, it is a topic that can't be avoided. For a small monthly fee there is even a paging service to inform you as soon as a high-speed chase breaks out so you can get off the freeway where it is taking place and dash to the nearest television screen.

Self-help

It is said that all Germans are ill, all Greeks are mercurial and all Danes healthy. Scratch the surface of any sportive, self-assured, Golden West trendsetter, and you are guaranteed to find a mental make-up fit for long-term therapy. Truman Capote said: "In California, everyone goes to a therapist, is a therapist, or is a therapist going to a therapist."

A very real effect of living within a delusion is the

insecurity of not measuring up to the image. Most Californians grow up in a world where bathing beauties and lifeguards swig beers, chomp burgers and gulp 'thirsty-two' ounce cokes as if there is no fat tomorrow. As far as television is concerned, these calories appear to collect solely in the chest area.

The plethora of self-help literature produced by Californians is not so much a reflection of their EQ as a constant and often redundant search for the answer to their question: "How come I'm not as good as on TV?" On the other hand, thanks to clever packaging and gimmicky marketing, life-advice and watered-down psychology are made accessible to just about everyone. Texts and concepts that baffle most students are transformed by Californians into easy reading. Jungian theory of archetypal ideas, when subjected to the Californian sun, re-emerges as *Soul Mates*, *Jesus CEO*, *Chicken Soup for the Soul*, *Anatomy of the Spirit* and '*EQ*'. It has been said that for every year you live in California you gain one point of EQ. (Rumour has it that it is paid for in loss of IQ, but that's beside the point.) The result is that many Californians are indeed emotionally aware. At least, they believe themselves to be. And as the delusion dictates, if enough people believe something, it must be true.

The Big One

Long before Charlton Heston and 'Sensaround', Californians were divining the coming of the Great Quake. Not a year goes by without the hysterical prophesising of family and friends over the date, time and epicentre of the earthquake that will make the one in 1906 in *San Francisco* (with Clark Gable) seem like a hiccup. Living as they do on the world's biggest fault-line, Californians have experienced seven major earthquakes since then.

There is a strange sort of acceptance deep down in Californians that the Big One must come and that they deserve it. But for those who choose not to take the fire-and-brimstone view, the idea of an earth-shattering jolt just adds spice to the delusion. *Carpe Diem*... This time tomorrow you might be swimming.

Behaviour

The Young

Young Californians grow up quickly, peak at around age 14, burn out at 19, acquire the legal right to drink alcohol at 21 and then proceed to spend the rest of their lives acting like 14-year-olds.

Most receive a rude awakening to adult life early on, as they observe their parents divorcing, claiming bankruptcy, struggling with drug addiction, getting thrown in jail, attending AA meetings, tattooing themselves and coming out of the closet. Before many kids are old enough to read the self-help books lying on the coffee table, they find themselves in the position of emotional caretakers to their out-of-control moms and dads who just can't get it together.

The resulting parental strategy for fathers is one of 'daddy and buddy'. The child is treated like a pal – a little peer who can help out when the going gets tough. It's a complicated relationship, which simultaneously nurtures and abandons the child who often gains a friend at the expense of a father. For mothers, the strategy can be described as 'big sis, little sis'. Here, the daughter serves as a source of lost youth to the ageing mother who desperately apes her child's every move, snatching up and imitating clothing, music and language. Although

Californian mothers and daughters appear as thick as thieves, the relationship often suffers from an underlying element of competition that leaves the daughter feeling overly flattered and under-loved.

It is not really surprising that, like Macaulay Culkin, some decide to divorce their parents.

The Elderly

"When female Californians reach the age of 25 they turn invisible", claims a 47-year-old beach babe hiding behind a tummy tuck, chemical peel, two face lifts and three liposuctions. When male Californians reach the age of 25 they turn out the lights.

Many fads come and go with Californians but ageing has yet to catch on. Since 1992, cosmetic surgery procedures have increased 153%. The 1972 film *Logan's Run* depicts a futuristic world where everyone is expected to liquidate themselves at the ripe old age of 30. Apart from not yet having constructed domes around the inhabited regions, this describes Californian culture quite well. The elderly who choose not to disappear – known as "Runners" – are forced to escape to sanctuaries like Palm Springs or Carmel where they can still turn heads with their cat-eye sunglasses. Those who cannot afford to escape attempt to disguise themselves as young people. These unhappy retirees are often at best marginalized, and at worst mugged.

Eccentrics

Californians have developed an ingenious way of dealing with eccentrics. Those with no money go to Berkeley or Venice Beach. Those with a bit of money go to San

Francisco or Hollywood. And those with a lot of money found churches.

Berkeley has attracted so many oddballs that it has earned itself the title "The Open Ward". On any given afternoon one can witness people kissing the pavement, screaming the word "rare", singing into invisible microphones, blowing bubbles, preaching salvation or ranting about conservative plots to end vegetarianism. It isn't called "Berzerkeley" for nothing.

Most Californians have such a deep affection for the unorthodox that given the chance they will often donate money to their cause. The most successful in this category have been those who use the word 'Jesus' in their ranting and ravings. Reverend Gene Scott (a spacey televangelist with beard and Greek sailor's cap) needs a staff of operators to collect all the gifts.

More often than not eccentrics are not just tolerated by Californians, but rewarded for their behaviour. They end up on postcards, in the newspaper, on television, and always with a crowd of supporters egging them on for more. This of course does not apply to places like Laguna Nigel where the suburban elite raises its young. Here the eccentric will be expeditiously apprehended and shipped off to Venice Beach where he or she belongs.

Minorities

In California everyone is a minority – indeed, every individual is a special interest group: the dog-walker who campaigns for playgrounds for pets, the sunbather who rallies for the right to nude recreation, the activist who supports the California Militia ("we are not a bunch of mad bombers"), or the waiter who joins the International Correspondence of Corkscrew Addicts.

The constant battle for attention amongst minority

groups is what keeps the minorities from becoming majorities. The bottom line is that nobody identifies with the norm, because that is the one group nobody wants to be part of.

Pets

The Californian dog holds a cherished position. In Sherman Oaks for $60 your pooch can have a one-hour 'touch therapy' session. Or a canine 'hydrosurge', or a hot-oil back rub or perhaps a 15-minute poodle snip for $44. Better still, it can receive a 'hands on' healing massage in which 'Chi' energy is run through it. This will cost no less than $45. It's a high price to pay for a display of wealth that really just wants to fetch a stick.

Leisure and Pleasure

Pumped Up

The words 'free time' are spoken with relish in California, and yet the concept of leisure in the sense of 'a time for ease without hurry' is ultimately frightening. As the reality nears, the Californian panics and seeks refuge in one of his or her endless high-speed virtual adventures.

LA alone boasts no less than four major amusement parks of the kind sought by Chevy Chase in *National Lampoons: Summer Vacation*, where your free time can make your work week seem like loafing. Life in the Bay Area is so rich with clubs, causes and organisations that one can make it through retirement without ever having seen an empty minute.

Sex

How many Californians does it take to screw in a light bulb? Californians don't screw in light bulbs; they screw in hot tubs.

Californians practise intercourse just about everywhere except behind closed doors. In any LA nightlife guide you are bound to stumble across the club called Fuck – it doesn't get any more direct than that. Hollywood Boulevard billboards bulge with mammary glands, the Castro with Dorian Grays and the beaches of Orange County with pubescent beauties struggling with their cultural obligation to wear that bikini top. Mr Zogg's Sex Wax, advertised as being "the best for your stick", is not something you buy at the drug store but something you use to get better traction on your surfboard.

Californians love sex – true, they love their hairdresser, Will Smith and jalapeño peppers as well, but sex is at the top of their list. Sex is the sublime topic – in Berkeley it's scrutinised, in Hollywood it's packaged, in San Francisco it's explored, on Vine Street it's sold, and in 'Sin' Valley, the G-spot of the blue movie industry, it's simulated. Porn stars like John Holmes become pop-icons and legitimate actors like Hugh Grant behave like porn stars.

In fact Californians are prudish at heart. In this respect – though they try to fight it – they remain as American as apple pie. They are continually trying to push the limits of sex – and many succeed – but the bottom line is that most do it with guilt.

Orson Welles, Hollywood's own *enfant terrible*, gave an interesting insight when asked about his experience in Tinseltown: "It's not about money – and it's certainly not about sex. They love to talk about it, but I never saw anyone doing it. It's about power – it's about who is considered number one this year." The actress Tallulah Bankhead was perhaps not alone when she said: "The conventional sexual position makes me claustrophobic – the others either give me a stiff neck or lockjaw."

Being sexy is part and parcel of being Californian. Actually enjoying sex is not.

Getting High

In a culture striving to be high on life, it should come as no surprise that drugs play a major role. Californians are passionate about drugs. They are either passionately for them or passionately against them. In both cases, it's a centre of conversation.

Alcohol is generally consumed abusively. Californian parties are not marathons, but hundred-yard dashes. For younger Californians, drinking is often a race against the police coming to crash the party. For older Californians, the 2.00 a.m. curfew on bars and clubs becomes a race against the clock.

Marijuana is against the law, yet Southern Californians prefer it to cigars and Northern Californians grow it like cabbage, often in underground farms to avoid detection. Cocaine – symbol of the LA pace of the '80s – is also against the law. There was a time when it was normal to see white lines at parties, and film stars had clauses in their contracts which guaranteed them a certain amount of "popcorn". Today it's considered old-fashioned in the face of everything from Ecstasy to LSD to crystal meth to bungee jumping.

In the end, Californians would just as soon go sky diving as smoke dope. It's not how you get high that is important, it's just important that you get high. Most Californians are publicly against alcohol and drug abuse. Alcohol is the social lubricant and moral solvent that usually opens the door to the bathroom where more interesting intoxicants are being taken. However, puritanical guilt slips in, and though Saturday night is a blast, Sunday morning usually entails a certain degree of down-to-earth remorse.

Personal Growth Weekends

Reflective of the Californians' need to 'get a grip' on reality is the popularity of what are called Personal Growth Weekends. For a price of between $300 and $500, Californians can spend a weekend self-actualising themselves. A spiritual cure might take the form of a Barbara DiAngelis' Making Love Work seminar or a visit to The Chopra Center for Well Being where the emphasis is on individual development, experimental processing and new awareness.

The Human Potential Movement, which began in the early '70s, is another phenomenon that can trace its early days to Californians. Werner Erhard's EST, which began life at Big Sur in 1971, was originally a 60-hour seminar where students had to surrender their watches, were not allowed to take breaks, and had to 'break down' the old before they could build up the new. It is based on the very Californian idea that self-actualisation can be achieved through subjecting oneself to demanding personal ordeals such as firewalking, glasswalking, or Rolfing (deep muscular manipulation that aims to provide the 'patients' with some form of personal epiphany while their bodies experience pulverisation of the sort undergone in the Spanish Inquisition).

The basic principle, therefore, of these Growth Movements is to dissolve the participants' conventions and conceptions of themselves. This is quite radical in contrast to Europeans who place a great emphasis on roles, i.e., a lawyer is not an archaeologist. The Californian would see the profession of lawyer or archaeologist as something more similar to a role in a film than a calling from God. A role is played as long as it is enjoyable and profitable. If lawyers were to fall out of vogue – something quite unlikely in the Golden State – then the Californian would pack up shop, return to university at the age of 52 and become something new. The Personal Growth Movement is born out of this attitude, and its weekends are designed to strengthen the individual's body and soul for such a change.

Holidays

Unlike, for instance, the Germans, who get six weeks' paid vacation per year, the Californians work hard for just two. The vacation is a cherished time when family and friends get the chance to wind down from the high-strung West Coast pace in a relaxing atmosphere like Honolulu, Acapulco or Mazatlan. Destinations such as Boston or Chicago, though acceptable for reunions, don't count as pleasure retreats.

As if the warm California sun wasn't enough, holidays must be spent where it blazes. Laughlin, Nevada, with annual temperatures hovering around 110°F (43°C) and a precipitation of zero, is a popular spot with Californians who seek the shade of their houseboats by day and second-rate casinos by night. The catch phrase for this holiday is "we're going to the river". The Californian is talking about the Colorado River, but don't expect a bird-watching hike. The trip inevitably entails jet skis, speedboats, barbecues and massive quantities of beer.

Some of those who take winter holidays spend them on the slopes of a ski resort near Lake Tahoe, Mammoth or Big Bear. But 90% of Californians spend Yuletide tanning themselves, lizard-like, on their patios.

The reality is that most Californians don't have holidays. The majority spread their precious free time across the year in the form of emergency trips 'back home' (i.e. Boston or Chicago) or extended weekends. Typical getaways include anything from a drive up, or down, the coast, to dropping in on Vegas to take in a show and roll the dice, fishing for White Marlin in Baja California, or simply being trapped at the toll booth of a bridge.

Sports

From the first prenatal bounce of Mother's aerobics to Grandpa's last power walk, sports play a central role in Californians' lives. Toddlers are throwing footballs before they can read and write. The same can be said of certain collegiate stars. In high school, youths spend up to five hours a day training for the glory of their alma mater and in the hope of becoming a pro. Homework is secondary.

Whether it be volleyball or rock climbing, surfing or racquetball, frisbee or lacrosse, Californians push themselves to their limits, which is what being Californian is all about. Women's soccer has grown with such popularity that children can't get a ride to their own games any more.

If Californians aren't playing, they're watching – either the game or the celebrities on the bleachers (cheap seats). Jack Nicholson is a manic basketball fan – LA Lakers – who are in turn his fans. Everyone is watching everyone else, which itself is a sport. However, if you doubt the seriousness of these spectators, ask people from Oakland what they thought of LA buying their football team. In fact, ever since the Angelenos bought the Brooklyn Dodgers and Cleveland Rams, the Southland has been making an art of corporate athletics.

In California, sports and the media are one of the few happy marriages around.

Culture

Culture Cult

California is a shining example of the fact that culture can not only be bought, but can be sold too. If America's greatest export is itself, Californians appear to be the ones most ready to wrap it up and ship it. How many New York films and sit-coms were actually shot in LA the world will never know – *I Love Lucy*, *Kojak*, *All in the Family*, *Taxi* and *The Jeffersons*, to name a few. Follow Broadway far enough and you'll end up on Sunset Boulevard every time.

Many outsiders have fallen prey to the view that the land of sea and sun is without Culture. They forget that a considerable portion of their own culture has come from or been influenced by these people who appear to value burnt dermis over grey matter.

The Californians have seized the world's cultural resources with some of the most unlikely of icons: from Pamela Anderson to David Lynch, Nathanael West to Harvey Milk, Bugs Bunny to David Hockney. Yet they possess an uncanny knack for transforming tradition into trendiness, history into happening, custom into culture. They are more than willing to admit they don't have any cultural resources, but they appear to have an understanding of culture the rest of the world has somehow failed to grasp.

To the student of Budapest's renowned Liszt Academy, classical music is the noble thread that stitches a thousand-year tradition to the present. To the Californian rap star, it's just another track to be sampled.

Japanese eat sushi – Californians 'do' sushi. They slip avocado into their roll of seaweed and rice and call it a "California Roll". They pour their saké into a beer and call it a "Depth Charge". To the Japanese, it's probably like painting a moustache on the Mona Lisa, but the

Californian will think it is better. It's somehow more fun.

In a world where so many passively look at a screen to share a rampantly spreading global culture, it's often forgotten that culture is something active. Californians, in all their delusional glory, are not afraid to pick up a guitar and make an absolutely terrible recording. They've also proved themselves worthy of writing uninspired books, launching useless products, creating concept-less art, developing unhealthy diets, producing mono-synaptic movies and founding meaningless religions – but they did it, and that's their secret.

Highbrow

Culture in the Californian sense can only exist in the present. Once it has been copied, it is transformed into tradition. History, on the other hand, is permanent and thus in conflict with the Californians' life-philosophy.

For example, the beautiful English town of Bath, steeped in history that flows back to before Roman times, at present produces very little culture in the Californian sense. Most of its trends come to it from Bristol, which looks to London, which rubs elbows with New York, which unsuccessfully tries not to be influenced by Californians. Meanwhile California continues to bombard the world with new trends and customs. (For example, the latest craze in tattooing, piercing and scarification can be traced to the 1980s' Modern Primitive movement in California. Bands like the Red Hot Chilli Peppers brought it mainstream. Samoan Californians of course were always doing it.) Bath is historic, Hollywood is cultural. Thus Californians prove to be surprisingly liter-ate regarding Quadrophenia, Pulp and The Verve, while thinking the Wars of the Roses was a movie starring Michael Douglas.

Custom and Tradition

Flags

Californians love flags. The passion is patriotically driven. With so many ethnic groups living in California, flags of all nations are to be found just about everywhere. There are shops filled with them. On Independence Day (the Fourth of July) the Stars and Stripes are proudly hung from almost every home and business. On Cinco de Mayo (Mexican Independence Day) the flags change in colour to red, white and green.

A current trend is 'house flags'. True to the Californian spirit of extroversion, most houses are fitted with 'pole-holders' for flags to show the occupant's interests. Mr Schatzberg waves a flag with an anchor so everybody can know about his yacht. Mrs Beaumont hangs a flag with a big Dalmatian. And the Gonzales family flies a pacifier (baby's dummy) to let the world know about its new arrival.

Christmas

Surprising to those from cooler climates is the fact that Christmas is the most Californian time of year. Irving Berlin may have been lamenting when he wrote 'I'm Dreaming of a White Christmas' during a sojourn in LA, but it's the yearning that makes it all so sweet (ask a Pennsylvanian what he thinks of snow).

It may be difficult to imagine palm trees dressed in garlands and lights, or Santa in shorts, but to the Californian it's magic. Indeed, magic is the best word to describe the transformation of a Mediterranean landscape into a winter wonderland. Of all the holidays Californians celebrate, Christmas is the least adapted to the West Coast climate and thus the best suited to a people who love to pretend. Aerosol snow is sprayed on windows. Elves are planted on lawns. Lights are hung on houses. Neon Santas and reindeers are mounted on rooftops.

Southern Californians bundle up as temperatures fall into the 60s (15-20°C). Northern Californians enjoy a few degrees less as chilly winter days tease the freezing point. Eggnog is drunk as every dropping degree is relished. Fires in fireplaces are lit. In fact, with the exception of the UK, the traveller will find more fireplaces in sunny LA than in most European countries. In this respect, the English-speaking Californians have retained a bit of their Anglo origins.

House decoration is of the utmost importance to the Californians who must drive to the mountains if they are to see any snow. To the outsider, the result may look like something out of a fantasy-horror comic book, but to the Californian it is a valid substitute for ice-skating in Central Park.

This pride in lights and elves is cleverly illustrated in the film *LA Confidential*. In the opening scene some undercover cops are about to raid a case of domestic violence in progress. As the camera follows them, you see a kitschy suburban home – inside which a man is beating a woman. The first cop to approach the house, instead of breaking the door down, reaches up to the large, blinking, plastic Santa's sleigh on the roof and rips it down. The wife-beater practically drops his victim on the floor as he rampages out of the house looking for the person who has just committed this most unpardonable sin.

The Californians' ability to produce the spirit of Yuletide is faithfully depicted in a little creation called *It's a Wonderful Life* directed by Frank Capra. Arguably the snowiest movie in the history of Hollywood, the cameras never left the studio during one of LA's hottest summers.

Another Californian variation on Noël is the Christmas

boat parade. Boats and yachts are dressed up to sparkling perfection and paraded around harbours where the reflecting water adds magical effect. Communities like Naples Island in Long Beach go to such lengths to decorate their boats and homes that during the holiday season they become local tourist attractions.

If you are not willing to accept fake snow and plastic Santas, then it is possible to visit Santa's Village near Lake Arrowhead in the San Bernardino Mountains. Here, amidst giant plastic mushrooms, an 'alpine' roller-coaster, a 'petting' zoo, peacocks and a lady who hands out free candy, young Californians can make their holiday requests to a real Kriss Kringle – give the beard a tug to make sure – and play in real snow.

Bachelor Parties

Californians may not like taking off their bikini tops, but hiring strippers is fine and dandy for parties – birthdays, office parties, reunions, conventions, and that critical ritual that all Californians sooner or later, usually more than once, pull through: the bachelor party.

Before a wedding takes place, by the unwritten laws of tradition, the groom-to-be is allotted one last night of drunken debauchery before settling down into matrimony. For Californians this entails one of three scenarios: drinking copious amounts of alcohol and going to a strip bar, drinking copious amounts of alcohol and hiring a stripper, or going to Las Vegas and doing both. The father of the bride is often invited to the event and is sometimes even present as Buffy-The-Melon-Queen does her thing at midnight.

This tradition is not one-sided. Californian women have developed the bachelorette party. This is basically the equivalent of the male version, but wilder. Here a team of Chippendale muscle men comes dancing into a living room which by this point in the party resembles a pit of lionesses. Only the strongest of males can actually handle this job. They will often dress themselves as policemen or cowboys in an attempt to intimidate the hungry pack. It never helps.

Eating and Drinking

The LA institution called The Pantry – never without a customer since 1924 – wraps its takeaways in paper that reads: 'Enjoy life: eat out more often.' These simple words capture the Californian philosophy for living – the secret to deep fulfilment. Ask any West Coast divorcee where to find that special meal and he or she will have the keys to the car out in seconds.

The choice of food is astounding: you can sample exquisite morsels daintily decorating a plate at Chez Bernice, or hot dogs from a stand shaped like a hot dog; beef that is raised in boutique ranches, or dim sum in Chinatown; tiramisu in Little Italy, iced coffee in Little Saigon, bulgoki in Koreatown, or soul food in Oakland.

In California, restaurants are more plentiful than trees. They are to the Californians what the bathhouse was to the ancient Romans. That is to say, the spot where almost all relevant familial, social and romantic interaction takes place. A visitor from Hong Kong, where culture places a high value on communal dining, was of the opinion that the Californians' inability to have a normal sit-down family dinner was at the root of their isolated and egocentric culture. A standard question on Californian psychological assessments is whether the client eats with his or her family. Perhaps what is really being asked is, can one enjoy life too much?

Red Hot Chilli Peppers

Although Mexican food has been trendy elsewhere in the US since the '70s, and in many European countries since the '80s, it has been the driving force of the Californian kitchen since the '90s – the 1790s.

Californians like their food spicy. Though the West Coast palate has expanded far beyond tacos and burritos, it remains true to all that is piquant. Be it Chinese red peppers, Japanese wasabe, Vietnamese sriracha sauce, French Dijon mustard or good old-fashioned Tabasco, the attitude is 'the hotter, the better'.

Even Bloody Marys are made so spicy, you'll forget you ever had a hangover as you desperately search for a glass of water. And though it wreaks havoc on the digestive tract, the pain of a sun-baked chilli pepper ultimately brands the Californian's identity. For no Californian when transplanted abroad will avoid withdrawal symptoms for warm tortillas, chile relleño and margaritas.

Many Californian adolescents go through the rite of passage known as the pepper-eating contest. As proof of their masculinity they will order bowls of fresh chilli peppers from their favourite Mexican restaurant and – not without sweat and tears – gulp them down. The prize is usually about $5 and maybe a free beer to put out the fire. The price paid for this display of manliness is nothing short of emasculation and a very unpleasant memory in the bathroom the next day.

Diet

Whereas nutritionists see diet as the food people eat, Californians see it as a milkshake, i.e., the food they don't eat.

The Californian diet is dictated by immigrants and an American attitude of abundance. In other words, one can eat just about anything all the time in double the portion.

Californians do not eat at certain times. They eat all the time. Restaurants and supermarkets remain open 24 hours a day. Breakfast can be eaten at 7.00 p.m. and dinner at 7.00 a.m. No-one will bat an eye. Indeed, try to eat a Harbor House Café omelette – consisting of six to eight eggs, guacamole, bacon, cheddar, salsa, toast and potatoes – in the morning, and you may not be able to bring your stomach to work.

Apart from round-the-clock restaurants and supermarkets, home delivery is common and fast-food drive-thru's are around every corner. The San Joachin valley is a cornucopia of produce, the Napa Valley a store of wine, and the Pacific Ocean a reservoir of seafood. If you're Polynesian you'll find kava, and if you're Cambodian you'll find durians. The difficulty with such an environment is staying thin within it, especially when the dominant culture demands that everyone looks like the 19-year-old lifeguard.

Californians have ushered in the health food, organic, vegetarian and vegan movements. In Berkeley there is the Berkeley Bowl – a bowling alley gone organic market – where one can find just about everything organic under the sun. Nevertheless, diet is ultimately in conflict with fitness for Californians. Bulimia is a familiar word to teenagers who all too often find themselves in all-night burger joints, their inhibitions numbed after hours of partying, chowing down on the food they denied themselves during the day.

The California diet is better spoken of in terms of quantity than quality. The quality of food is good, but the problem is everyone eats too much. In other parts of the world this could be seen as healthy, happy or wealthy, but the Californians end up in a schizophrenic state of bingeing and purging as they unsuccessfully try to enjoy life to the fullest while remaining fit.

Health

Get Fit

It's not whether they're healthier than other people that Californians care about. It's the rush that counts: the runner's high from a gush of endorphins to the brain causing it to forget the unpaid credit card bills. Fitness is fashion – something to flaunt like a brand new car. It's an integral part of the superficial world that moulds the Californian ideal. It gives the illusion of prosperity a physical form and proves to Californians that they are somehow better.

The irony is that Californians have created a world where fitness plays no role whatsoever. The car has replaced the legs, restaurants have replaced farms and sports bars have replaced sports. Fitness has become more a response to a crisis than a genuine desire for health. Thus Californians go about their fitness desperately, drive the car to the beach – finding a parking place as close to the sand as possible – and then run for their lives during the 30 minutes that have been allotted to staying "tight".

Hygiene

When Californians get 'dressed to the teeth', they mean it. Quality dentistry is abundant, as evidenced by all the dentists in quality cars. Dental hygiene is linked to external appearance and is therefore of considerable importance to Californians who will generally visit their dentist more often than their priest.

Each practice has a hygienist (usually a beautiful young woman) who will give you fluoride treatments and a Hollywood smile with a show of ivories that could compete with Liberace's Steinway.

Hygiene is respected and upheld in all sectors of public life with the exception of the sea. All is not as it might appear on the cosmetic sands of *Baywatch*. Bathers may bring home more than a tan after a long day at the beach, by way of skin rashes and eye infections. In the murky depths of the Pacific, Californians get away with hygienic murder. They have not gone so far as to invent words for these silent infractions of nature's law – as have the Australians who contributed the term 'Bondi cigar' to the English language – but they are guilty just the same.

Business

In LA, Russ Meyer may have produced films entitled *The Valley of the Dolls*, but what has been called the Valley of the Dollars is nearer San Jose. This apposite epithet refers to Silicon Valley, birthplace of three of the world's most powerful computer companies – Hewlett Packard, Apple and IBM – and a slew of other internet entrepreneurs who are changing the planet at light speed.

In fact the South Bay, where the cost of a house doubles the American national average, is home to more than quarter of a million millionaires and is said to produce no less than 64 new millionaires every day. Jerry Yang is one of them. Born of Chinese immigrants, he is co-founder of Yahoo!, creator of *Jerry's Guide to the Worldwide Web* and at twenty-something is a multimillionaire.

Producing software is an essentially Californian endeavour, i.e. it's non-reality-based. The great holdings of Silicon Valley have not made their fortunes from the production of computers, but from ideas to organise computers better. Californians may abide by the American work ethic, but nothing beats innovation. Their strength is creative, their skill conceptual. In places like Stanford, new thoughts are worked into shape like the biceps on Muscle Beach.

Californians might look as if they're having fun, but in fact they're working their butts off. In the free-for-all market that is the internet, foldout desks and caffeine pills provide the backdrop for 80-hour work weeks and 17-hour days. Passion is the buzzword used to describe the ascetic devotion to becoming the next Amazon.com. Discussing the relationship between a non-existent love life and the thrill of launching a new web site, Calvin Lui, Chief Executive Officer of a cyber dating service, simply concludes: "I'm married to this now."

In no better realm than business can one witness the physical manifestation of the Californians' many delusions. In most places variety is the spice of life. In California it's a commodity. Amidst the concrete jungle of West Coast trade, competition is fierce and business justifies its existence by the great Darwinian principle of survival of the weirdest. One burgeoning case in point is HardArt, which for a sizeable fee will replicate your phallus for posterity. *The Chicken Boy Catalogue for a Perfect World* offers everything from toothpick holders to underwear, all with their distinctive hen-headed Elvis logo. A California dream is not something to be analysed; it's something to be sold.

Players

It is an age-old mistake to interpret a Californian's lack of formality as a lack of expertise. In fact, most Californian professionals possess what could be called 'the secret weapon'; that is to say the hidden arsenal of knowledge and vocabulary that only comes out under duress. A Californian may dress like a Grateful Dead fan and may talk like a teenager, but when it comes to doing business, a surprisingly well-prepared Jack will pop out of his box bringing his Stanford Doctorate along with him.

It's confusing to Californians themselves in professional relations. Ninety-nine per cent of the time all is fun and games, but the other 1% should never be forgotten. Shining smiles are quickly eclipsed by the cold shadow of reason when it's time to discuss the results. And like the rugged individuals they aspire to be, colleagues will denounce their own brothers if a job is not done well.

Government

Protest is Best

Californians feel strongly about their government. Most feel strongly that they need a new one.

Within a five-day period in 1988, they watched Jesse Jackson, America's first black presidential candidate, call for his Rainbow Coalition in Berkeley, and George Bush, standing next to Chuck Norris and the Beach Boys, cry out "Read my lips, no new taxes" in Modesto. Both were met with loud cries of support.

Californian political issues oscillate between fiscal conservatism and social liberalism. Reagan's tax-cutting propositions are rooted in Southern Californian Republicanism, and yet the same people support abortion – a fact that keeps campaigners on their toes. Only three times in the past century has a presidential candidate reached the White House without winning in California, testifying to the power of the West. Due to California's influence on the rest of the country, it is US government policy that California serve as the last stop on the presidential campaign trail.

While other parts of America are demographically greying, Californians are getting younger and browner by the day, living in a place more multi-ethnic than other states will be in 50 years' time. The result is simple. As Californians continually change, so do their politics – a situation perfectly suited to a people fascinated by an uncertain future and forgetful of its past.

Politics

In San Francisco, Jello Biafra, head of the punk group The Dead Kennedys campaigned for Mayor and didn't do too badly. In the film *Play Misty for Me*, Clint Eastwood's character is stalked in Carmel, and some 20 years later he was running the place. Sonny Bono in his post-Cher years ended up as the Mayor of sunny Palm Springs.

Orson Welles once considered running for Governor in his native Wisconsin against none other than Joseph McCarthy, but thought that a Hollywood divorcee could never get elected. If they had been running in California, where a Hollywood divorcee named Ronald did just fine, America might have avoided one of its darkest moments in history, the anti-Communist trials of the 1950s.

Probably the most successful Californian in politics has been child star Shirley Temple (married to diplomat Charles Black) who for 40 years has been a US ambassador. Jane Fonda forged a career spanning *Barbarella*, Vietnam protests and aerobics. Warren Beatty, who played a gangster in *Bonnie and Clyde*, made a film in 1999 about a rapping politician, and then considered running in 2000 for President.

Richard Nixon, who was a native Californian, made history by charming the Chinese and failing to charm the Americans. His retirement was spent in Orange County frequenting Mexican restaurants in San Juan Capistrano.

Californians love a good show, and they expect this of their politicians. Flamboyance and eccentricity are by no means a deficit in Californian politics. As far as the debate about 'art imitating life' or 'life imitating art' goes, the latter rules in the Golden State.

Systems

Dealing with Extremes

Most of the time Californian weather is warm and inviting: "Clear and sunny", "Clear and sunny", "Chance of a cloud", "Clear and sunny". About once every 80 years LA gets some snow – not really enough to make a snowman, but enough to throw a snowball – and the news cameras broadcast it nationwide.

But when it does change, it does so like the wrath of God. Ocean storms strike with ferocious winds and crashing waves that destroy piers and take lives. In spring, the Santa Ana winds from Mexico blow strong and hot, rendering the land a veritable match waiting to be struck. Freak fires reduce hillsides of houses to ashes in minutes, and torrential rains cause mudslides that swallow highways and demolish million-dollar homes. The street-wide cement storm-drains of LA (which provide such dramatic movie backdrops for scenes like the drag race in *Grease* and the bike chase in *The Terminator*) may seem too big for the trickle of water running down the centre, but these silent witnesses to the variable weather of a desert are just a thunderstorm away from becoming a raging river.

Californians deal with all this surprisingly well. When a catastrophe hits, it's usually turned into a media event, and the Californian once again gets to be the centre of attention, often exaggerating the danger to unsuspecting family members in other parts of the country. For life in California is not the Russian roulette that the world thinks it is. The greatest damage caused by the Loma Pieta quake was financial, not fatal. And most Angelenos experienced the worst of the 1994 Los Angeles earthquake via the television screen like everyone else. Earthquakes and floods are real, but the daily life-threatening danger of them is really part of the myth.

The Blue Line and BART

Possibly the most shocking realisation a visitor will have upon reaching California is that public transport does exist. The Californians themselves are more often than not the guilty parties who perpetuate the illusion that the pedestrian is extinct in the West.

The entertainment industry and City of Los Angeles have invested the sum of one billion dollars in the redevelopment of Hollywood and the Southland. The jewel of the crown will be LA's Union Station, which already stands as a major architectural attraction for those who appreciate Art Deco. Hollywood Boulevard will have a metro running beneath it. The Blue Line, already in action, is an urban railway system which begins on the streets of Long Beach and ends in marble-paved subway stations under downtown Los Angeles, with enough armed guards patrolling the compartments to cause a cardiac arrest if you're caught just trying to sneak a free ride.

Visiting the Bay Area for the first time could lead one to believe that 'Bart' must be the most popular guy around. It's not unlikely that an attractive woman at a café in the Mission District will say "I'm taking Bart to the movies tonight". In Oakland, a handsome man may exclaim "I'm taking Bart into the city". If you live anywhere near San Francisco, Bart is your best friend. It's the abbreviation of 'Bay Area Rapid Transit' – a tidy, French-designed, suburban train reminiscent of the Paris RER that beats the pants off waiting in a car to get across the Oakland-Bay Bridge during rush hour.

School

School is a highly variable experience for Californians. The city of Long Beach, hoping to bring back the good old days, reinstated its law requiring uniforms to be worn in all elementary schools. High schools in the same city require gun and knife searches.

The Mentally Gifted Minor (M.G.M.) Programme suggests that all Californian kids are not created equal. Based on IQ levels (which are evaluated at the ripe old age of five and facilitate a European cultural background), it gives young Californians the chance to be bussed to special schools where they spend their childhood believing they are better than other children (a.k.a. "normals"). It is indeed a shock for the "mentally gifted monkeys" (as they are called by the 'normals') when they enter high school to realise they are no more intelligent, nor better prepared, than the rest. The system reveals much about the underlying elitism of California.

To all intents and purposes, a California elementary education is perfectly suited to the individual who wishes to become a con-artist, pop icon or professional athlete. Reading, writing and arithmetic seem nothing more than necessary hindrances to the extracurricular activities that dominate Californian education.

The situation is worsened in high school where a championship football game can bring in crowds numbering tens of thousands. The Latin Club will never see such popularity. Surfers and pop musicians, though on the fringes of high-school culture, also end up with perks the bookworm could never dream of. It's always possible that Mom and Dad's little pot-smoking nightmare – though a failure in chemistry – will find himself on the cover of international magazines if he's willing to get up at 6.00 a.m. every morning to catch some waves before class. Meantime, the young Californian would-be movie star moonlights as a stand-in for videos in Hollywood. His grades may be disastrous, but when he pops up on television as a student drop-out in *Beverly Hills 90210*, all is forgiven.

University

The wonderful thing about living in a delusion is that genius is not reserved for the elite. For the 32 million dreamers living in La-La Land, there are no less than 106 Universities and Colleges backed by another 107 Community Colleges where, for around $75 a semester, the only requirement is to have reached the age of 18.

In contrast to the all-American stereotype of ivy and brick at $8,000 a semester, California is filled with education bargains. Of the dozens of Californian Nobel Laureates, a significant 32 taught in the state's public university system. A Bachelor's Degree in Science at Berkeley in the 1960s could be taught by no less than 12 past and future Nobel Prize winners. In its heyday California managed to make genius public property. Today it turns it into Silicon Valley whiz kids.

Though it may seem extraordinary to outsiders, the Californian miraculously becomes quite serious at university. Students at the Sorbonne may have murals painted by Chagall in their lecture halls, but the Californians have silence. It's as if they have subconsciously realised they got away with intellectual murder for the first 20 years of their lives and it's now time to catch up. While the French and the Japanese work frenetically before finally making it into university, at which point they go wild, the Californians experience the opposite.

Cops and Court

Breaking the Law

Crime is wrong – any Californian will agree. The problem is defining what a crime is. Taking drugs is a crime. And yet in Berkeley they hold periodic "Smoke-Outs" where marijuana is handed out and puffed and blown at the police who look on. Speeding is a crime. And yet try to drive the 55-mile-per-hour speed limit on an LA freeway without getting rammed from behind. Prostitution is a crime. And yet North Beach is filled with bathhouses and Sunset Boulevard with a lot of suspicious-looking women. Police brutality is a crime. And yet, in spite of what was seen on the video, all four police officers were acquitted in the Rodney King case. Murder is a crime. And yet O.J. Simpson managed to be judged guilty in one court and innocent in another.

Of course, some laws are taken quite seriously. Smoking, for example, can bring down the wrath of the the state in a moment. A Long Beach billboard showing an enormous burning cigarette reads: "This weapon kills from both ends" – apparently worse than a gun, which kills from only one end. And in California you are in a state which does not allow you to buy alcohol until you're 21. In fact, you aren't allowed into any establishment where alcohol is freely served without proof of your age at the door – valid identification (for a citizen) or a passport (for a visitor). And if you think Californians are as relaxed as they look on television, try showing up at a popular club and explaining that you simply left your ID at home, even if it's obvious that you are 40 years old and won't cause the management any problems. Time and again guests are turned away after an hour's wait, politely instructed to return to their hotels, read a copy of the California Penal Code, and return with the all-important validation.

Cops

Controlling teenage mischief comes hauntingly close to a Sam Peckinpah film in which the police force suburban delinquents to lie on the ground, faces in the dirt, handcuffed as if they were wanted dead or alive. But as long as *Starsky and Hutch* still make the late-night re-runs, Californian cops will probably continue to treat their job like a Western. Perhaps due to their child-like nature, Californians prefer the strong-armed approach to law enforcement. Cops are everywhere. They're on the beach wearing shorts. They're on the street using rollerblades. They're in neighbourhoods on bikes. They motorcycle the freeways. They shoot you with radar. And they buy up all the best doughnuts.

Unlike the Dutch police, who will turn their cheek to most infractions that don't hurt anyone, California's finest will almost scare the poor jay-walker to death before he makes it to the other side of the street. Alfred Hitchcock, who already had a fear of police when he arrived in California, found a mother lode for his phobia. The cop who casually interrogates Janet Leigh in *Psycho* embodies the fear that all Californians feel every time they are stopped for something they have no idea they did.

The only thing worse than cops in California is imagining the place without them.

The Media Made Me Do It

For every Californian on the screen, there are 32 million others vying for the spot. All Californians, consciously or subconsciously, dream of fame.

Cary Stayner, the motel handyman charged with the brutal murders of four women near Yosemite National Park, is one of them. Expecting that a 'movie of the week' be made of his terrible deeds, he offered to split the profits with his victims' families. Early on, Stayner learned that actions are judged by their capacity to raise ratings, and only the most extreme are rewarded with media coverage.

Kody Scott met fame in prison by writing a book called *Monster: the Autobiography of an LA Gang Member*. The secret to his success is not so complicated as one might think: "I get these ideas from watching movies and watching television." In his conception of gangs it's not the crime that counts, but the reputation: "If the media knows about you, damn, that's the top."

For image-oriented Californians, crime is arguably nothing more than a means to the greater end of being seen and recognised. The state keeps producing police when it is paparazzi that the people want.

Court

With a divorce rate of 50%, a passion for small claims and a proclivity to injury when it's not their fault, precious few Californians have avoided the courtroom. As if there was a strange sort of love for the place, they are always on the lookout for a lawsuit that will bring them (once again) into the courtroom. Life's path is littered with trademarks, copyrights and warnings on products which reflect lawsuits of yore: "Do not pour cough syrup into eyes", or "Peanuts contain nuts".

If it is brought to the attention of a waiter in Greece that a hair has been found in your salad, he will pick it out for you and ask if he can help you in any other way. In Germany, you will be asked to prove it was not yours. In California the crisis must be handled with the utmost care: the waiter's friendly smile will not mask his fear. He knows a hair can cost millions. Usually with hushed apologies, the meal will be offered gratis, or some similar gesture will be made, for it is the restaurant's desperate desire to settle out of court.

The passion to hear the knock of the judge's hammer is enhanced by a tidal wave of television shows. Re-runs of Perry Mason, Californians' favourite TV-lawyer, compete with shows like *People's Court*, *Divorce Court* and *Judge Judy*. Change channel and you might end up with *Law and Order* or *LA Law* (arguably an oxymoron). Thanks to cable television there is *Court TV*: 24-hour-a-day coverage of everyone's problems but your own. There is even *Judge Wopner's Animal Court* if pedigree disputes are your thing.

Many of these programmes are interrupted by your local attorney at law advertising the cheapest divorce rates, name changes, or procurement of green cards in town. That is, if he isn't out 'ambulance chasing' – getting the injured to sign up as new clients so that someone can be taken to court.

Conversation

Californians are basically very open people. More often than not, they'll share their problems with you as easily as their successes. Taboos centre on prying into or challenging someone's delusion. If Jack tells you he's going to start a surfboard company, don't bring up the fact that banks don't give loans to McDonald's employees. And if Dwayne tells you he's going to be a rap star, don't mention the negative odds – give an example of someone who hit the charts.

It's quite appropriate to ask someone how much he makes; however, one should not delve too deeply into how it was made. If it's from illegal drug dealing, or working 16 hours a day at the hardware store, your interest could accidentally offend him as he enjoys his 15 minutes of stardom.

Language and Ideas

Foreign Languages

Of the many foreign languages spoken within California's borders, English is the most popular. It's the primary language of instruction, though many schools have integrated Spanish, California's first foreign language, into their curriculum.

Most English-speaking Californians live out their lives in a state of ignorant bliss regarding the Spanish world in which they live. They argue about the possibilities of a bilingual society without even glancing at their own addresses – some 80% of the place-names are Spanish. Most have forgotten that Spanish was being spoken in California long before the Yankees wandered in from the East. Many more don't realise that, next to Mexico City, LA is the second largest Mexican city in the world. And Spanish is now the first language of more than a quarter of Californians.

The majority of Californians may be speaking English,

but words such as *dinero, cerveza, loco, mucho, amigo, barrio* and *que pasa** have become vernacular standards in the West Coast tongue. Bank machines, telephones, television, radio and public forms and services already offer Spanish. Famous Spanish-speaking Californians like Cesar Chavez already grace textbooks and Boulevards. From Ricky Ricardo to Ricky Martens, their voice has rung in the ears of Californians in denial of the multi-lingual world in which they live.

Pre-contact California was one of the most linguistically diverse regions in the world with over 300 languages. Even before the Europeans came, Californians were trying to outdo everyone else.

For a linguist, visiting the California Department of Motor Vehicles (DMV) is akin to being a kid in a candy store. Here – to name a few of the languages on the information rack – one may learn how to drive in English, Spanish, Mandarin, Cantonese, Cambodian, Vietnamese, Korean, Armenian, Samoan or Tagalog.

Speaking Californian

The Californians' particular form of English broadcast into homes across the globe is at once the world's lingua franca and incomprehensibly provincial. The linguistic irony is that though the world is connected to Californians, they remain cut off from the world. The mountains and desert to the East are still a very real barrier between Californians and the rest of America. Crossing the Pacific to Japan is not like crossing the Rhine into France. Californian language reflects this isolation.

In the dearth of contact with the rest of the world, Californians are left to invent new words all on their own. San Franciscans have adopted the word 'funky' to

* money, beer, crazy, a lot, friend, neighbourhood and what's up.

signify everything from a house to a stomach ache. It usually connotes something creative or out of the norm – which all San Franciscans see as good. Angelenos, following the ancient American tradition of superlative language, enjoy exaggerated words like 'awesome', 'radical', and 'major'. 'Bogus' and 'bummer' express feelings of disappointment.

Black Californians are particularly active with their speech – they create new words and terms at such a rate that they struggle to keep up with themselves in communicating, like the rappers who sing about 'Cali', 'Dena', 'Oaktown', 'Strong Beach', 'Frisco' or 'West Side'. They are in fact talking about California, Pasadena, Oakland, Long Beach, San Francisco and the West Coast.

A Hispanic Californian once said: "You call me cool – I call you a *culo*!" *Culo* means 'asshole'. It pays to have friends outside your ethnic group.

That's All Folks

For the majority of the world, Californians don't really exist. They are nothing more than ephemeral images on a screen reacting to situations that could never take place, living on the spoils of an unobtainable dream, speaking a language at once exaggerated and cryptic. For the most part, the same is true of the Californians themselves who speak of their culture with the scepticism of an outsider.

Yet it has been these people – none of them aboriginal, and many not American – who built the factories and concepts that today service not just America, but the world. California may be a delusion, but it's a delusion shared by real individuals whose predecessors came for gold. It's a real delusion. And the Californians' delusion becomes everyone else's reality.

Have a nice day.

The Author

Anthony Marais was born in Hollywood the year Walt Disney died. His childhood was spent in Huntington Beach and Belmont Shore, doing what Californians do best: having a good time and not worrying about the future. In the 1980s he co-founded the Los Angeles pop group 'The Squids', a career move that effectively ended his future. He therefore went to Berkeley and found a new one.

An anthropologist and avid film collector, he claims to be on a campaign to promote dreaming and escapism as the only hope for achieving self-actualisation. The result has been a vagabond lifestyle of writing between Polynesia, Canada, France, Germany and California – one that has, as yet, brought him nowhere near self-actualisation.

He openly admits to loving both San Francisco and LA, the former in his opinion being archetypically Californian and the latter quintessentially American. Be that as it may, he claims it's the tacos that keep him coming back.